W9-BJM-262

DISCARDED

AFRICAN-AMERICAN INVENTORS

African-American Inventors

by Patricia and
Fredrick McKissack

A PROUD HERITAGE

The Millbrook Press, Brookfield, Connecticut

Photos courtesy of the National Portrait Gallery: pp. 12, 17; Historical Society of Pennsylvania: p. 22; Linda Whyte Burrell: p. 25; Library of Congress: p. 28; The Schomburg: pp. 31, 49, 52, 57, 64, 70, 89; U.S. Patent and Trademark Office: pp. 36, 37, 39, 46, 76; Bettmann Archive: pp. 43, 74; New York Public Library Picture Collection: p. 54; Henry Ford Museum & Greenfield Village Research Center: p. 59 (neg. no. B87109); Western Reserve Historical Society: p. 80; Wide World: p. 87.

Published by The Millbrook Press
2 Old New Milford Road, Brookfield, Connecticut 06804

Library of Congress Cataloging-in-Publication Data
McKissack, Pat, 1944–
African-American inventors / by Patricia and Fredrick McKissack.
p.   cm.—(A Proud heritage)
Includes bibliographical references and index.
Summary: African-Americans have produced inventions that made major contributions to a range of fields, often in the face of enormous obstacles and often with scant recognition. This book presents the stories of some of these remarkable men and women.
ISBN 1-56294-468-1 (lib. bdg.)
1. Afro-American inventors—United States—Biography—Juvenile literature. [1. Inventors. 2. Afro-Americans—Biography.] I. McKissack, Fredrick. II. Title. III. Series.
T39.M45 1994   609.2′273—dc20   93-42625   CIP   AC

CONTENTS

ACKNOWLEDGMENTS

A book of this kind is always difficult to write because of the volume of information that must be gathered, verified, organized, and then written. For raw data and date verification we relied heavily upon Vivian Ovelton Sammans's lists in *Blacks in Science and Medicine*, and Lerone Bennett's *Before the Mayflower: A History of Black America*. Also invaluable were the work of Portia P. James, curator of the Smithsonian exhibit, "The Real McCoy: African-American Invention and Innovation, 1619–1930," and *Black Inventors of America*, by McKinley Burk, Jr.

We would like to thank the Associated Publishers, Inc., of Washington, D.C., founded in 1920 by Carter G. Woodson, who made available all the articles written about African-American inventors and their inventions and also provided an extensive bibliography on the subject, compiled by Janet Sims-Wood, Assistant

Librarian, Moorland-Spingarn Research Center, Howard University, Washington, D.C.

We extend a special thanks to our friends and family for their help with this project and to our editors at Millbrook, who gave us the opportunity to document the lives of these great African-American inventors. Finally, we must thank the inventor of the fax machine, for without it this book would still be a "work in progress."

Patricia and Fredrick McKissack
St. Louis, Missouri, 1994

INTRODUCTION

In 1903 Henry Ford produced and sold the Ford Motor Company's first automobile, which he advertised as "a thoroughly practical car at a moderate price" of $850. That same year, Edwin S. Porter, one of Thomas A. Edison's directors, presented a twelve-minute motion picture entitled *The Great Train Robbery*. Marie and Pierre Curie were awarded the Nobel Prize in physics for their investigation of radioactivity, and on December 17, 1903, the Wright brothers, self-taught mathematicians and machinists from Dayton, Ohio, unlocked the mystery of flight at Kitty Hawk, North Carolina.

At the same time these important breakthroughs in technology were being made, a Maryland politician claimed in a speech that the "Negro is not entitled to vote because he has never evidenced sufficient capacity to justify such a privilege, because not one black person [has] ever yet reached the dignity of an inventor."

Even as this man spoke, Granville T. Woods, a mechanical engineer, and Lewis H. Latimer, an electrical draftsman, both African-American inventors, were actively involved in developing improvements to the electric light bulb (with Thomas Edison) and the telephone.

By then history had been so distorted that most Americans—black or white—weren't aware of the accomplishments of Africans in astronomy, mathematics, architecture, navigation, medicine, and agriculture. Even in America, black inventors and their inventions were not widely publicized, so they remained unknown to the general public. Often their contributions were ignored by white "authorities," omitted from history books, or blatantly credited to others. To further complicate matters, the United States Patent Office, unlike most other government agencies, had a long practice of not listing an inventor's race.

Even so, in 1900, Henry E. Baker, assistant examiner of the United States Patent Office, had painstakingly researched and compiled a four-volume series, listing several hundred patents granted to black scientists and inventors, dating as far back as 1821. Another list, published in 1913, contained over a thousand names. These lists offered conclusive proof that black men and women had consistently received patents for a long time on machines, new chemical compounds, foods, and medicinal products, as well as on the processes for producing them.

In *African-American Inventors* we have tried to place African-American inventions within the larger context of American history and to show how they helped improve the lives of people everywhere. Although the men and women in this book labored under the tyranny of slavery, oppressive segregation, and overt racism, they were still achievers. Some died in poverty, a few amassed fortunes, but they were all successful. No matter what their circumstances, all of the inventors presented in this book are important American heroes and have earned the right to be remembered. They continue to inspire new generations of inventors and entrepreneurs.

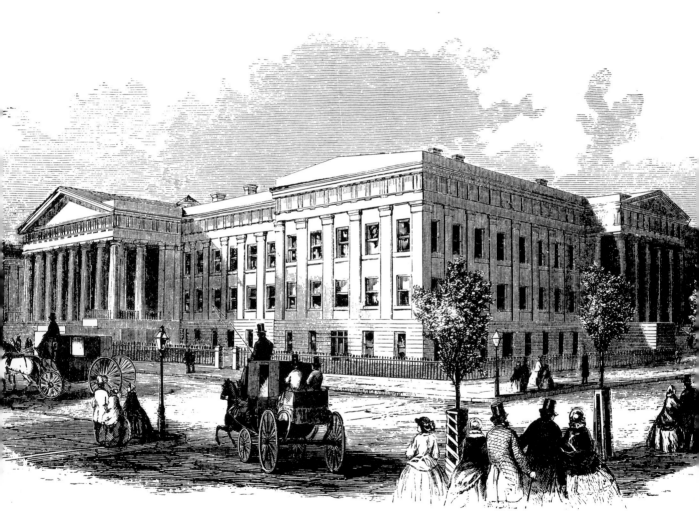

The U.S. Patent Office in 1869.

1

PATENT HISTORY
AND LAW

Inventors are people who develop, improve, or find
new uses for machines, manufactured products, or industrial processes. To invent is to create a device or
process that has not existed before. To innovate is to
modify, change, or improve an existing design. Most of
the time inventors protect their inventions or innovations by applying for a patent.

A patent is a document issued by the government,
granting an inventor the exclusive right to make, use,
and/or sell his or her invention for a period of time,
during which the patent holder is protected from theft
or unfair use. Thomas DeForest, author of *Inventor's
Guide to Successful Patent Applications*, explained government patent policy as follows:

*The Federal Government grants patents to encourage
and reward the creation of new technology. This is the*

deal: if you invent something new and agree to tell every-one how to make and use it, then you get monopoly rights for 17 years. During this time, you can sue anyone who makes or uses the invention without your permis-sion, and (hopefully) collect money from people who do have your permission.

History of Patents

The idea of patents didn't originate in America, but in Europe, during the Renaissance. Before that time, European countries had very few laws that protected the inventor's ownership rights. Unless inventors were wealthy and powerful, their work was very often stolen or exploited by monarchs, patrons, or church officials. Unprotected inventors rarely got credit or fair compensation for their labors. In fact, during the Dark Ages, European inventors often found themselves on the wrong side of religious doctrines of the day. Some people were hauled before the Court of Inquisition because they were considered "too clever."

In China cleverness was revered and inventors were encouraged. In the Middle East, North Africa, and other Islamic countries, inventors were considered vessels through which Allah channeled special gifts to mankind. Although Islamic inventors were highly honored, it was an unacceptable idea that any person was capable of "invention," which was closely associated with creation. Our word "discovery" is the word that best suits the Islamic notion of invention.

The earliest known European patents, called "privileged grants," were issued to inventors in Florence, Italy, sometime in the early 1400s. A time period was placed on the exclusive rights of the holder to avoid the creation of monopolies.

The history of American patent protection begins in 1641, when Samuel Winslow was granted the first patent letter in the colonies. It protected his unusual way of processing salt. The Puritans of colonial America discouraged "tinkering," for fear it was "sponsored by the devil." But the framers of the United States Constitution believed patent protection was important.

The Constitution states:

The Congress shall have power . . . to promote the progress of science and useful arts, by securing for limited times to authors and inventors the exclusive right to their respective writings and discoveries.

President George Washington signed a bill for a patent system on April 10, 1790. At that time, the granting of patents was placed in the hands of the secretary of state, the secretary of war, and the attorney general. Thomas Jefferson, who was himself an inventor, examined many patent petitions for "useful art, manufacture, machines, or devices as they should deem sufficiently useful and important."

At one time, all a patent applicant needed to do to get a patent was pay a $30 fee and swear he or she was the inventor. There was no examination process involved. Then the United States Patent Office was set up on July 4, 1836, and the position of "commissioner of patents" was created by Congress. When the Department of Interior was established in 1849, the patent office was moved to that agency. It stayed there until 1925, when President Calvin Coolidge issued an executive order moving the patent office under the Department of Commerce, where it remains today.

The patent office developed strict guidelines, some of which are still in force. Inventions fit into one of five categories: process, machine, manufacture, composition of matter, or improvement. A *process* is a method of doing something—for example, a special way of putting together a bed.

Machines are devices that have moving parts or that transform forces, such as the telegraph, television, or a pencil sharpener or a shoe-lasting machine. A *manufacture* is an article or object that does not have moving parts, such as carbonless copy paper. Inventions in the category of *composition of matter* consist of human-made chemical mixtures and compounds, including such things as insect repellent, shaving cream, and cereal. An *improvement*, or innovation, improves upon or changes the use of an existing process, machine, manufacture, or composition of matter. For example, an inventor you'll read about in Chapter 4 built a machine that improved the way sugar was refined in the nineteenth century.

When an inventor builds on the work of others, improving or modifying existing designs or processes, patent examiners are required to check carefully for "prior art" to make sure the inventions are more than an obvious variation of a previously existing design. They also want to make sure that the changes are substantial enough to merit a new patent.

For a long while, inventors were required to submit a "working" model, along with their applications, but that is no longer necessary. Rough drawings are acceptable, but the applicant must "clearly describe

Patent examiners review applications from inventors. During the 1800s, applicants were required to submit models as well as drawings of their creations.

how to make and use the invention" and define exactly what is new about the invention and what makes it different from what has been invented before. Finally, examiners check to see if the invention or innovation is operable and useful.

In the early years, it was easy to test a design or process to see if it worked, but usefulness was subjective and therefore more difficult to prove. Often disputes over usefulness had to be settled in court.

In 1817, a patent case regarding usefulness reached the Supreme Court. Justice Joseph Story interpreted useful to mean the invention was "not frivolous or injurious to the well-being, good policy, or sound morals of society." Justice Story's decision remains the standard by which usefulness is defined today.

Africans arrived in the New World with knowledge that they used in farming, toolmaking, and medicine. Since the patent office did not exclude free blacks or slaves from receiving patents, many African Americans applied for and received patent protection for a wide variety of products and processes.

SETTING SAIL ON
A STORMY SEA
Free African-American Inventors

Prior to the Civil War, most African-American patent holders were free. They had an outlet for their creativity. Working every day with tools and machinery gave them the opportunity and the incentive to discover new ways of doing things and improving upon others. A majority of free blacks worked as either domestics, laborers, skilled artisans, or seamen, so the things they invented are primarily in these areas.

The Contributions of Free African Americans

Thomas L. Jennings (1791–1859), believed to be the first African American granted a patent (on March 3,

1821), developed a turpentine-based fluid used to clean clothing. Jennings became a successful businessman and used a large portion of his profits to support the abolitionist movement—a cause to which he was firmly committed. (Some standard reference books name J. B. Jolly, a Frenchman, as the first person who started a laundry where a turpentine solution was used to dry clean clothing in 1855.)

Between 1800 and 1860, the United States was basically divided into two camps: abolitionists and slaveholders. At the core of the controversy was always the question of black intellect. Slavery advocates argued that black people were incapable of the kind of problem solving it took to become scientists, physicians, and inventors. But abolitionists used as their strongest defense the accomplishments of free blacks such as Benjamin Banneker, a scientist; Martin Delaney, a physician; and Henry Blair, an inventor.

Blair, described as ''a successful Maryland farmer,'' was granted a patent for a corn harvester on October 14, 1834, and another one in 1836, a year before John Deere manufactured the first steel reservoir plow.

Another African American, George Peake (1772–1827), settled in Ohio about 1809, where he made a hefty sum from a stone hand-mill he invented.

Several important black abolitionists came from the ranks of seamen. John Mashow of South Dartmouth, Massachusetts, became a well-respected shipbuilder who designed his own ships. He ran his own company from 1831 until just before the Civil War, and used his wealth to support the antislavery movement. Paul Cuffee was a ship's captain and shipbuilder who went to sea at age sixteen. By twenty-five he was captain of his own ship, a twelve-ton vessel manned with an all-black crew. He made voyages to Europe, Russia, Africa, and the West Indies. In 1797, Cuffee built a wharf and warehouse and joined in the fight against slavery.

By 1800 there were several thousand black seamen employed along the eastern shore from Maine to Maryland. Among them were two inventors whose influence on the maritime industry and ideas about slavery were revolutionary: James Forten and Lewis Temple.

There is an old seaman's warning that one should never set sail in a storm, but James Forten (1766–1842) didn't take that advice. He developed a sail-handling device that was particularly useful in rough waters and built a lucrative business around his invention. Among the free black inventors of the early American period, Forten is probably the most recognized.

Forten learned about sails when he enlisted in the navy at age fourteen during the American Revolution. He served as a powder boy aboard the privateer *Royal Louis*, but it was captured in battle and Forten, along with twenty other crew members, was taken by the British as a prisoner of war. Forten was later released.

After the war, he returned to Philadelphia, the city of his birth, and became an apprentice to a sail maker, Robert Bridges, who had also employed Forten's father. At age twenty, Forten was foreman of the crew, and by 1798, he had become the owner of the sail-making business. Shortly afterward, Forten developed his sail-handling device, but he never patented it. The exact date of his invention, therefore, is unknown.

Forten was an outspoken critic of slavery and Northern racism and discrimination and he took action

An outspoken opponent of slavery as well as an inventor, James Forten would not install his sail-handling device on any slave ships.

against them whenever he could. Two unsuccessful slave revolts, in 1800 and 1822, contributed to the popularity of the American Colonization Society, which stated that free blacks were "a dangerous and useless element" and should be sent back to Africa. In 1817 Forten drafted a statement that the free blacks of Philadelphia submitted to the state, denouncing the American Colonization Society.

Whereas our ancestors (not of choice) were the first successful cultivators of the wilds of America, we their descendants feel ourselves entitled to participate in the blessings of her luxuriant soil, which their blood and sweat manured; and that any measure or system of mea-

sures, having a tendency to banish us from her bosom, would not only be cruel, but in direct violation of those principles, which have been the boast of the republic. . . .

Captain Cuffee, however, supported a back-to-Africa movement, and in 1816 he used his ship, *The Traveller*, to transport thirty-eight blacks to Sierra Leone in West Africa.

Forten also wrote a series of letters to the Pennsylvania State Congress, the governor, and other leaders, attacking the arguments of whites who wanted to limit the number of free blacks entering Pennsylvania. Forten donated a sizable amount of money in 1831 to William Lloyd Garrison, who published *The Liberator*, an antislavery newspaper. As soon as he took over the sail-making business, Forten refused to rig slave vessels with sails. He organized other businesses to boycott them as well.

Lewis Temple (1800–1854) also added his voice to those of the New England abolitionists. Temple was born in Richmond, Virginia, but he fled to New Bedford, Massachusetts, as a young man. By 1836 he had opened a metal-working shop where he did repair work for whalers. Later, he moved his blacksmith's shop to the Walnut Street Wharf. Abolitionists often met there to discuss the treatment of black seamen, especially in southern ports. In Charleston, South Carolina, for example, black sailors were forced to stay in jail until their ships sailed because the residents feared the sailors might lead a rebellion and use their ships to transport slaves to freedom.

At other times the sailors talked about the problems they had with their equipment. At that time, a whale was killed by using a barbed spear with ropes attached. Once the whale was speared, the crew used smaller boats to get in close for the kill. But sometimes the barbs didn't hold and the whale got away.

This is what gave Temple the idea to improve upon the harpoon. The toggle harpoon he designed and made changed the whaling industry almost overnight. This harpoon entered the whale's flesh and locked in place. In many ways the toggle harpoon was a reinvention of a concept that had been used by ancient fishermen. They used a similar device to spear and hold large fish until they could be killed. Temple didn't patent the harpoon, so immediately other blacksmiths began to copy and sell his design.

Unfortunately, one night Temple stumbled over some loosely secured boards at a city construction site, fell, and severely injured himself. He sued the city, and on March 18, 1854, the Common Council awarded him $2,000 for personal damages. He died a month and a half later, leaving a $1,500 estate. According to a newspaper account, he never received any money from the judgment. Neither did his widow and children.

Free Blacks in Business

Sometimes slaves waited until they were free to develop the ideas they had formulated while in slavery. The work of runaway slaves served the abolitionists well because it was tangible evidence of what free people might be able to accomplish.

John Parker (1827–1900) was hired out by his master to work in an iron foundry in Mobile, Alabama.

*In this sculpture by James Toatley, Lewis Temple
is shown with the toggle harpoon he invented.*

Hired-out slaves were assigned by their masters to work for another person, but the master received the wages. In addition to his normal workload, Parker worked overtime and holidays for two years and earned $1,800, enough money to buy his freedom. As a free man, he moved to Ripley, Ohio, in 1850, where he became involved in the Underground Railroad, a system that helped runaway slaves get to freedom. Empowered by his freedom, Parker used the skills he had learned as a slave and invented a tobacco screw press in 1854. The function of the screw press was to compress the tobacco leaves into a more manageable bundle for shipment. He manufactured it at the Parker Machine and Foundry Company, which stayed in business until the end of World War I.

Although Northerners were generally against slavery, there were more than a few who advocated segregation. There was a lot of resentment, particularly toward skilled blacks who challenged whites for jobs in business and industry. To keep white workers from rioting or striking, many Northern businesses adopted the policy of hiring whites first and then, if there were still jobs available, offering them to blacks. In the case of layoffs, blacks, regardless of seniority, were let go first. Thus the saying: blacks were the last hired and the first fired.

Naturally, these unfair hiring practices resulted in the underemployment of skilled black laborers. To compensate for this, some blacks started businesses of their own and hired other blacks, and sometimes whites, to work for them. Less enterprising whites were frightened and angered by these independent free blacks, as the story of Henry Boyd (1802–1886) shows.

Like John Parker, Henry Boyd earned his freedom by working double duty as a cabinetmaker's apprentice and in the saltworks near his home in Kentucky. In 1826, he went to Ohio, where at first he was refused a job. He eventually found work as a carpenter, and used his carpentry skills to develop a new wooden bed frame. The bed has been described as "constructed so that its wooden rails could be screwed into the headboard and the endboard simultaneously, creating a stronger frame." He manufactured the Boyd Bed at his factory in Cincinnati, Ohio, until 1863.

Researcher Portia James noted that Boyd didn't patent his bed frame, choosing instead to seek "indirect protection" for it in 1833 "by having a white cabinet maker receive the patent for him."

Other furniture builders copied Boyd's design, but he stamped his name on each bed he made. Boyd employed up to fifty employees and ran a clean, safe shop. But arsonists twice burned his factory, and twice he rebuilt it. In 1863, Boyd finally had to close his doors when he could not buy fire insurance.

Today Boyd's beds have great value as antiques, and museums all over the world seek to include one in their collections.

It is a fact that free blacks who had more education, more time, more mobility, and more control over their lives were able to patent more inventions than slaves. But that is not to suggest that slaves were less creative or incapable of being inventors.

Benjamin T. Montgomery, who invented a boat propeller,
could not obtain a patent because he was a slave.

THEY WERE
THE FIRST
Slave Inventions

A few masters allowed their slaves to apply for patents, but the slave owner still remained in control of the patent licensing and profits. Therefore, there was little or no motivation for slaves to be creative. The records show, however, that slaves were active inventors and innovators, motivated by the need to make their work easier or safer. Portia James, author of *The Real McCoy*, cites these early examples: Ebar, a slave in Massachusetts, invented a new technique around 1800 for making brooms from broom corn. An Alabama slave, Hezekiah, invented a cotton-cleaning machine around 1825; and an unidentified slave in Kentucky is said to have invented the hemp-brake machine.

Locating and verifying information about inventions made by slaves is very difficult. Information about their inventions is particularly hard to find because often masters made minor modifications on slave designs and claimed them as their own. Slowly, researchers are uncovering information about slave inventors. This material is sometimes found by chance in letters, diaries, and other sources that were not intended to be used as documentation for slave inventions. As facts are made available, the picture becomes more focused. Some researchers, for example, believe Eli Whitney's idea for the cotton gin and Cyrus McCormick's harvester were inspired by slaves.

James stated:

Cyrus McCormick's harvester was primarily inspired by his slave assistant, Joe Anderson. While Anderson himself is not recorded as claiming sufficient role in the conceptualization of the reaper, he worked closely with McCormick during its construction. Anderson does say that he served as "blower and striker" for the blacksmith who made the harvester . . .

Eli Whitney has been charged with borrowing the idea for the cotton gin from a simple comb-like device that slaves used to clean the cotton. Whitney is said to have merely enlarged upon the idea of the comb to create the cotton gin, which works very much like an oversized comb culling the seeds and debris from the cotton.

Technically, Whitney and McCormick didn't do anything illegal. Basically, all inventors are part of a living chain, each one building on the work of others' "discoveries, formulas, principles, techniques, and mecha-

Eli Whitney's famous cotton gin, like most inventions, was based on earlier ideas.

nisms.'' Slave masters, however, often took credit for or benefited from work that was not their own, as in the case of Stephen Slade.

Slade, a North Carolina slave, was in charge of his master's tobacco farm. His work included growing, harvesting, and curing the tobacco. One day in 1839, Slade was curing a batch of tobacco. The leaves were hung over hot coals until they were dried to a deep brown shade. Slade fell asleep, and when he woke, the fire had almost gone out. To his surprise, the slow, smoldering fire had turned the leaves yellow. Slade decided to let that batch of tobacco cure slowly, which turned the leaves a rich, golden color instead of the dry brown. When the yellow tobacco was taken to market, it brought four times the usual price. "As a result," wrote James, "Stephen Slade's owner became the most celebrated tobacco grower in the Virginia-Carolina area and was often sought after for lectures and agricultural conventions on tobacco-curing techniques." One has to wonder what he talked about, since he had taken no part in the growing, harvesting, or curing of the tobacco.

The Dred Scott Decision

During the 1850s, the conflict over slavery further divided the nation. The Kansas-Nebraska Act opened the northwest territory to slaveholders, and the enactment of a second Fugitive Slave Law allowed slave owners to come into free states to recapture runaway slaves. These laws endangered the stability of free African-American communities all over the country. While some blacks fled to Canada and Europe, where slavery had been abolished and they could live without fear of being recaptured, others decided to return to Africa. It was a terrible time, made worse by the Supreme Court's decision in the Dred Scott case. Abolitionists were certain then that slavery wasn't likely to end without armed conflict.

Briefly, the case involved a slave, Dred Scott, who sued for his freedom, based on the grounds that his master had taken him to live in a free state. If slavery was not permitted in the state, Scott's lawyer argued, Scott should be free. Opposing lawyers argued that slaves were property no matter where their masters took them. For example, if a person took a horse into another state, wouldn't the horse still be his property?

A lower court ruled in Scott's favor, but the Missouri Supreme Court overturned the decision. The case was then argued before the United States Supreme Court. On March 6, 1857, two days after James Buchanan was inaugurated as president, Chief Justice Roger B. Taney handed down the 7–2 opinion of the majority in the Scott case.

Taney stated that black people were not citizens of the United States. They were property and, therefore, they had no rights in America which white people "were bound to respect."

In the eyes of the highest court in the land, African Americans were classified as property, along with horses, cows, and household furniture. This time the Supreme Court decision affected both free and enslaved blacks, because the court stripped them both of citizenship privileges. As the decision was interpreted, even free blacks could not vote, hold office, or receive a patent.

Up until that time, patent laws in the United States had protected inventors and their inventions regardless of race, sex, or social status. After the Dred Scott decision, patent laws no longer applied to blacks—free or slave—because they were not recognized as citizens.

Southerners were pleased when they heard the results of the Dred Scott decision, but they weren't thinking of how the narrow interpretation of the decision might backfire on them. One example involved Joseph Davis, the brother of Jefferson Davis. Joseph Davis owned Benjamin T. Montgomery, a slave who invented a boat propeller. Joseph and Jefferson Davis tried to have the propeller patented, but the patent was denied, because, according to the patent office examiner, Montgomery was not legally a citizen, which is a requirement for patent approval.

Later, when Jefferson Davis became president of the Confederate States of America, he recommended to the confederate Congress that a law be passed granting patents for slave inventions as long as they were controlled by the master. In part, the confederate law stated:

In case the original or discoverer of the art, machine, or improvement for which a patent is solicited is a slave, the master of such slave may take an oath that the said slave was the original and on complying with the requisites of the law shall receive a patent for said discovery or invention, and have all the rights to which a patentee is entitled by law.

There are other stories that illustrate how the Dred Scott case backfired on slaveholders who wanted to exploit the inventions of their slaves for personal gain.

A blacksmith named Ned, who was owned by Oscar J. E. Stuart from Holmesville, Mississippi, developed a cotton scraper that his master tried to patent. Stuart couldn't acquire a patent because he couldn't truthfully certify that the invention was his own. After several court appeals, the patent was denied.

When the Civil War ended, Ned disappeared, but Stuart's family started a business manufacturing the invention, which they named "Ned's Double Cotton Scraper." A customer wrote a letter to Stuart praising him for producing a slave invention because, the customer said, it "gave the lie to the abolition cry that slavery dwarfs the mind of the Negro. When did a free Negro ever invent anything?"

African-American Ingenuity

After the Civil War, Congress amended the Constitution, ending American slavery and declaring black people citizens of the United States with equal rights and protection under the law. One of the first places free blacks exercised their freedom was at the patent office. An unprecedented number of patents were issued to blacks between 1865 and 1900, many for inventions that were the forerunners of commonplace items used by millions of people all over the world.

David A. Fisher, Jr., invented a furniture caster (March 14, 1876, patent #174,794) that was a great improvement on previous designs. Today people can move refrigerators, pianos, and couches easily with the aid of casters.

William B. Purvis patented a number of devices that are still being used. He developed a hand stamp (February 27, 1883, patent #273,149), a hand-held device with letters carved in rubber and attached to a handle. Pens of the time had to be repeatedly dipped in ink, so Purvis developed a "fountain pen" (January 7, 1890, patent #419,065) with a container inside that could be filled with ink. The ink automatically flowed into the point, making it unnecessary to dip a pen into the inkwell after writing only a few words.

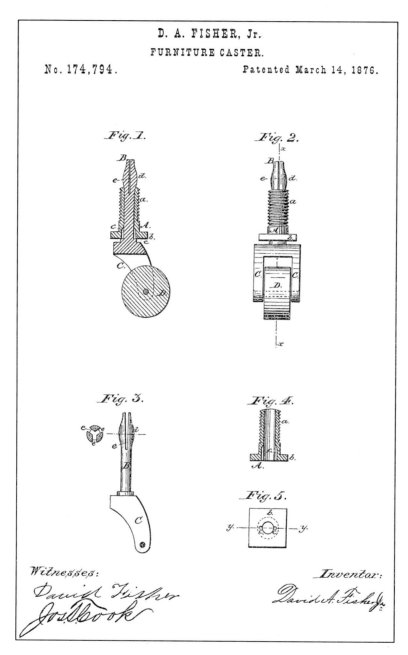

D. A. FISHER, Jr.
FURNITURE CASTER.

No. 174,794.

Patented March 14, 1876.

Fig. 1.

Fig. 2.

Fig. 3.

Fig. 4.

Fig. 5.

Witnesses:

David Fisher

Jos. T. Cook

Inventor:

David A. Fisher Jr.

David A. Fisher's caster could be screwed into furniture legs.

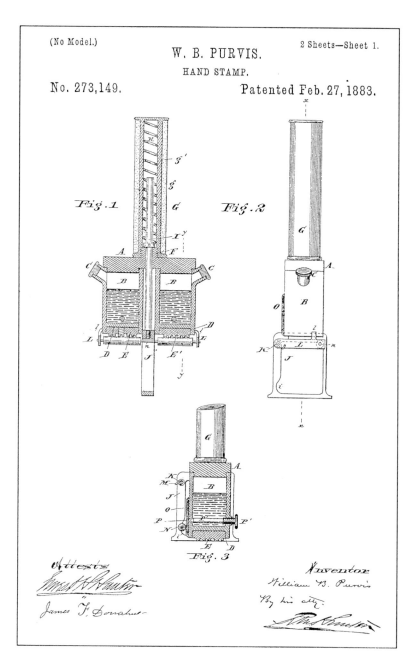

William B. Purvis's hand stamp had a reservoir for ink (B).

J. L. Love, who did a lot of writing, was slowed down every time he had to stop and whittle a sharp point on his pencil. He invented a pencil sharpener, patented on November 23, 1897 (patent #594,114). It was much like pencil sharpeners of today—a mechanical device that cut thin slices of the pencil away until a point was formed.

Both free blacks and slaves did much of the scrubbing, cleaning, cooking, sewing, and ironing for the wealthy class, so numerous household items were the result of African-American ingenuity. Imagine making a cake without an eggbeater. W. Johnson's eggbeater (patented February 5, 1884, patent #292,821) looked much like a modern-day whisk. It helped make preparing food much easier, and so did J. Lee's bread-kneading machine, patented August 7, 1894 (patent #524,042).

Lee, who worked in a bakery, knew how hard it was to pull, push, and turn the bread dough in the process called kneading. He developed a machine that "mixed, rolled and molded the dough in one operation." In 1895, he also patented a bread crumbling machine (patent #540,553).

There were very few women inventors, and very few of them were black. But some African-American women did make contributions. Sarah Boone, for example, invented an ironing board (April 26, 1892, patent #473,653) especially designed for the fitted clothing of the day. Sarah Good (Goode) received a patent for a folding cabinet bed in 1885 (patent #322,177), and in 1896, Julia Hammonds developed a yarn holder (patent #572,985).

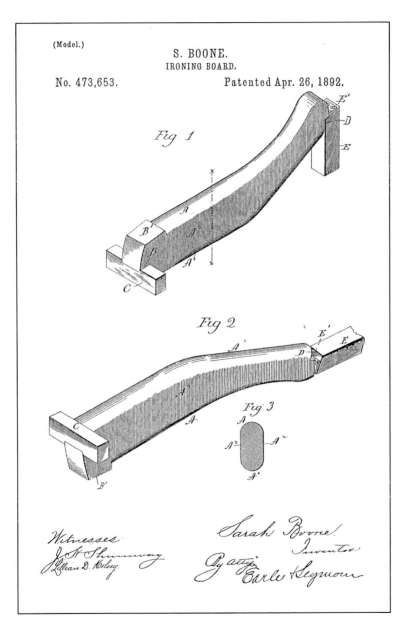

(Model.)

S. BOONE.
IRONING BOARD.

No. 473,653.   Patented Apr. 26, 1892.

Fig. 1

Fig. 2

Fig. 3

Witnesses
J. H. Shumway
Lillian D. Riley

Sarah Boone
Inventor
By atty
Earle Seymour

*Sarah Boone's ironing board was perfect
for fitted sleeves and bodices.*

Thomas W. Stewart knew how backbreaking it was to scrub a floor on his hands and knees, so he invented a mop (June 13, 1893, patent #499,402) with absorbent cloth attached to a handle; with it a person could wipe up a floor while standing upright. L. P. Ray patented an industrial-sized dustpan (August 3, 1897, patent #587,601) for picking up large amounts of trash.

George Grant enjoyed playing golf, but he had trouble keeping the ball from rolling when he tried to hit it. He invented a tiny wooden peg with a rubber top called a golf tee and patented it on December 12, 1899 (patent #638,920). Placed on top of the tee, the ball was held stationary for the first long drive, now known as the "tee off."

Bicycles were popular in the 1890s. People used them to run errands, but it was difficult to carry things and steer at the same time. J. M. Certain designed a basket (December 26, 1899, patent #639,708) that was attached to the handlebars and was the forerunner of today's bicycle carriers.

The inventions of other African Americans had far-reaching effects, sometimes even changing entire industries. In particular, the sugar and shoe manufacturing industries of the late 1800s owed their success in part to the inventions of two pioneer African-American inventors: Norbert Rillieux (pronounced REEL-you) and Jan Ernst Matzeliger (pronounced Mat-ZEL-i-ger).

4

SUGAR AND SHOES
Norbert Rillieux and Jan Matzeliger

Norbert Rillieux (1806–1894) invented a sugar-refining process that revolutionized the way sugar was produced. In a November 3, 1894, issue of *The Planter*, a nineteenth-century agricultural journal, an article praising Rillieux stated he was one of the most distinguished engineers who has ever been identified with the sugar industry. Although Rillieux's system was considered by those in the industry to be "the foundation for all modern industrial sugar evaporation," very few people knew he was an African American.

The making of sugar can be traced back to about 3000 B.C. in India. A general who traveled with Alexander the Great in the fourth century B.C. wrote about a "reed that produced honey without the aid of bees." In Sanskrit, a very old Indian language, the word for sugar was *sarkara*; in Arabic, it became *sukkar*. Rillieux, who grew up speaking French and English, called it *sucre* and *sugar*.

Christopher Columbus's voyages opened the Americas for European exploration and exploitation. Land speculators immediately took advantage of the myriad opportunities so vast a land offered. The balance of rich soil, sun, and rain was perfect for sugarcane growing, especially in the Caribbean and South America. The need for a large labor force to work the huge sugar plantations fueled the slave trade.

In 1737, sugarcane growing began in Louisiana, a French colony at the time. It was not until 1791, however, that the sugar crops became profitable. By 1806, the year Rillieux was born, sugarcane was the dominant Louisiana crop.

A Sweet Invention

Norbert Rillieux was born March 17, in New Orleans. Rillieux was a free-born black who, according to his birth record, was "the natural son of Vincent Rillieux a Frenchman and Constance Vivant, a free mulatto woman." The child was baptized in St. Louis Cathedral by Père Antoine and given the name Norbert Rillieux.

Vincent Rillieux was an engineer and inventor who developed a steam-operated cotton baling press that was installed in a cotton warehouse on Poydras Street. Norbert was bright and quick to learn, and his father was proud that his son was interested in machines and how they worked. Vincent sent Norbert to Paris, where his son could be educated without racial restrictions.

In this scene of the Louisiana sugar harvest, cane is cut, bundled, and carted to the refinery in the background.

After graduating from college, Norbert taught applied mechanics at L'Ecole Centrale in Paris, where he distinguished himself as a scholarly writer. In 1830, he published a series of widely read and respected papers on steam engine work and steam economy.

His interest in building a sugar-processing system began when he studied French sugar refineries. Having grown up in New Orleans, Rillieux knew how important sugarcane was to the area's economy, but American sugar refining was slow and tedious and also very dangerous.

The cane was boiled in big open kettles. Then it was purified by straining the juice to separate it from the cane. The liquid was evaporated by boiling it at very high temperatures; the granules that were left formed sugar. For years engineers in the business had been experimenting with ways to evaporate the cane juice safely.

The first sugar-refining system was introduced in France in the early 1830s. Sugarcane and beets were processed into sugar by using a steam-operated, single-pan vacuum evaporation system, which was a faster, safer, and more efficient procedure. Rillieux believed the evaporator system could be substantially improved.

He made plans to build a multiple-pan vacuum evaporator system, but his early efforts were only marginally successful. When he couldn't interest French machinery manufacturers in sponsoring his invention, he taught school to finance the project himself.

Several years later, a beet-sugar factory installed one of Rillieux's multiple-pan evaporators. It proved to be a very efficient way of processing sugar, and an improvement over the single-pan method.

Edmund Forstall invited Rillieux to come to New Orleans to be the chief engineer of a sugar refinery he was building. The deal fell through when Forstall had a disagreement with Vincent Rillieux, and Norbert sided with his father. Forstall fired Rillieux and the two men remained enemies for years.

Rillieux remained in New Orleans, but he left engineering and ventured into land speculation, making what some have called a small fortune. Unfortunately, he lost it all in a bank failure in 1837. Once again Rillieux returned to his sugar-refining invention, hoping for a breakthrough.

After a few setbacks, Rillieux finally got the chance he had been waiting for. Theodore Packwood allowed Rillieux to upgrade the refinery at his Myrtle Grove Plantation.

Packwood's operation had depended upon slave labor to transfer the boiling sugarcane juice from one steaming kettle to the next with long-handled ladles. With Rillieux's system, one workman could manage the valves that transferred the juice through the equipment as the cane was processed into sugar.

Based on Rillieux's design, a triple-pan evaporator was built by Merrick and Towne of Philadelphia and installed at Myrtle Grove Plantation. The system worked, and Rillieux patented it in 1843 and another improved version in 1846. (The Dred Scott case had not yet been decided by the Supreme Court.)

In a 1943 article in the *Negro History Bulletin*, Rillieux's system was described as the first multiple-pan evaporator patented in the United States. With Rillieux's system, sugar was refined by boiling the syrup into granules in two or three "vapor-heated vacuum pans." The system was faster and less costly, and the quality of the sugar was finer.

Rillieux's success was immediate and widespread. In 1846 several other factories installed his system, and eventually the boiling of sugarcane in open kettles gave way to his improved machinery. In 1849, thirteen sugar houses credited Rillieux for the increased sale of sugar.

Not satisfied to rest on his laurels, Rillieux turned his attention to another problem. He designed a way to

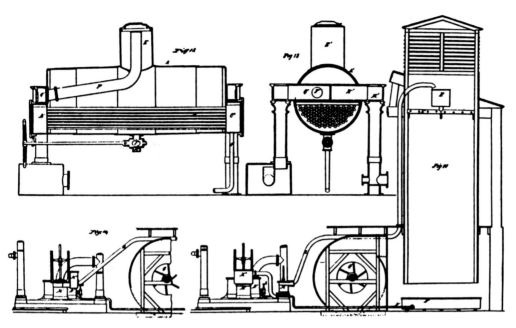

Norbert Rillieux patented this design for
an evaporating pan in 1846.

drain the lowlands around New Orleans, which were a
breeding ground for disease-carrying insects. The
Rillieuxs' old enemy, Edmund Forstall, was a member
of the state legislature and he opposed the plan. Although Forstall's motivations were personal, he was
able to sway others easily because of the growing resentment against free people of color in New Orleans.

To add to these problems, Rillieux was faced with
patent troubles back in Europe. The U.S. patents were
issued to him, and he alone benefited from the use of
his inventions in America. But a man who was working
for the Philadelphia firm that constructed Rillieux's
evaporators copied the drawings and took them to a
factory in Magdeburg, Germany. From the stolen de-

signs, the first European multiple-pan evaporator was installed at a beet sugar factory in Quincy, France.

The machines operated so poorly that they became the joke of the industry. A detailed account of the swindle appeared in *Evaporation in the Cane and the Beet Sugar Factory* by Edward Koppeschaar, published in London in 1914. Koppeschaar noted that the difference between the evaporators made from the stolen plans and those made in America by Rillieux himself was "his knowledge of the underlying scientific principles." The *Negro History Bulletin* stated: "A study of the text of these patents shows that [Rillieux] had a thorough grasp of both the theory and practice of multiple-effect (pan) evaporation."

Rillieux remained in America until after the Civil War, but then he returned to France. He had many interests that kept him physically active and mentally alert.

In 1880, a friend from Louisiana visited Rillieux in Paris to find him deeply involved in Egyptology. On the eve of his seventy-fifth birthday, Rillieux left for a visit to the pyramids. In 1881, he patented an improved version of a refining system that reduced fuel consumption. He personally supervised its installation in Egypt.

By all reports, Rillieux stayed busy until he died at age eighty-eight. His wife, about whom very little is known, buried him in a vault in the churchyard cemetery Père Lachaise in Paris, France. She lived until 1912 and was then buried beside her husband.

Few twentieth-century reference books included Norbert Rillieux's contribution to the sugar manufacturing industry. Those that did failed to mention that he was an African American. Yet, Charles A. Browne, a well-known sugar chemist of the Department of Agriculture, stated, "I have held that Rillieux's invention is the greatest in the history of American chemical engineering and I know of no other invention that has brought so great a savings to all branches of chemical engineering."

A Revolution in Shoes

Sidney W. Winslow, owner of the United Shoe Machinery Company in Boston, also boasted about the contributions of another African-American inventor, Jan Ernst Matzeliger (1852–1889).

Winslow wrote in his autobiography, published in 1917, that his company employed 5,000 people and represented the consolidation of over forty subsidiaries. His company, he said, was made possible after he bought the rights to use a shoe-lasting machine patented by Matzeliger, a black man. Winslow further described how his company had benefited from the Matzeliger machine:

The wages of workers greatly increased, the hours of labor diminished, and the factory conditions surrounding the laborers immensely improved. The improvement thus brought about in the quality and price of American shoes has made the Americans the best shoe people in the world.

This was quite a tribute to a man whose invention, when first introduced, was called "the machine" by angry workers who were unhappy about losing their jobs to a machine—especially one made by an African

Jan Matzeliger revolutionized the
shoe industry with his invention.

American. And what of Matzeliger? Sadly, he was unable to accept either praise or blame for his accomplishments, because he had died before he could enjoy the fruits of his labor.

Jan Matzeliger's shoe-lasting machine was the dream of a young man born in 1852. In the same year, Martin R. Delaney (1812–1885), a physician, inventor, and social activist, was denied a patent because he was not considered a citizen. Delaney's device was designed to assist trains in ascending and descending steep slopes. Delaney was so disappointed, he left for Central

America in search of more opportunities available to black men. He later returned and fought for the Union Army during the Civil War and earned the rank of major.

Matzeliger, who was born in Dutch Guiana (now Suriname) in South America, the son of a Dutch engineer and a Surinamese woman of African descent, came to the United States seeking opportunity. The Civil War was over and the newly freed slaves were taking advantage of the freedom and citizenship they had been granted by the Thirteenth, Fourteenth, and Fifteenth Amendments to the Constitution.

For a while, Matzeliger worked as a shoemaker's apprentice, first in Philadelphia and then in Lynn, Massachusetts. He learned to make shoes the way people had done it for centuries—by hand. Shoemakers pounded the leather with a stone to soften it. Next, they cut the leather, then stretched it over a wooden mold called a *last*. They punched holes in the leather with an awl and sewed the shoe to the sole.

Handmade shoes were so expensive, only the wealthy could afford more than one pair. Poor people wore ill-fitting hand-me-downs or no shoes at all.

By the 1880s many handcrafted goods were being manufactured by machines that produced more things faster and more economically. There were machines then that cut, sewed, and tacked shoes. But shoemaking had not been industrialized totally, because nobody had invented an automatic shoe-lasting machine that attached the upper portion of the shoe—the form—to the bottom part—the sole. Such a machine would be able to cut the production cost of shoes in half.

Matzeliger devoted every hour he could spare to working on an idea for a shoe-lasting machine. Each time he thought a design had been perfected, something went wrong. But Matzeliger wouldn't give up. He worked during the day at a shoemaker's shop, and spent the evenings poring over his model, often forgetting to eat or take care of himself. He felt he was close to achieving his goal, but he needed more time. Matzeliger quit his job and devoted all his energies toward his machine. When his money ran out and his health began to fail, he turned to two businessmen for help: C. H. Delsnow and M. S. Nichols.

Each man bought a third of the shares in the invention. With some financial security now, Matzeliger labored on.

Finally, in 1882, Matzeliger's machine lasted seventy-five pairs of shoes. Success! He applied for a patent right away, but the mechanical drawings were so advanced and the process so complex, the examiner could not verify if the machine worked or not. An examiner from the patent office visited Matzeliger, who personally demonstrated how his machine worked.

Nervously, Matzeliger put the parts of the shoe in place. The machine took over from there. It gripped and pulled the leather down around the heel, guided and drove the nails into place, and finally discharged the completed shoe. Jan E. Matzeliger was granted a patent on March 20, 1883 (patent #274,207).

Unfortunately, thirty-seven-year-old Matzeliger died of tuberculosis in 1889, four years after Martin Delaney had died in Pittsburgh where he had practiced medicine since the Civil War ended. Matzeliger had

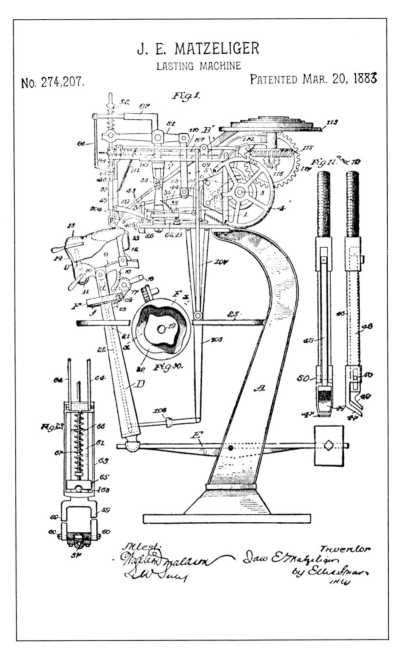

Matzeliger's lasting machine was patented in 1883.

been able to do something Delaney had been denied: obtain a patent on his invention.

Matzeliger was never able to enjoy any financial rewards for all his work. Since he never married, he willed his third of the shares in his invention to friends and to what is now the First Church of Christ in Lynn, Massachusetts.

Jan Matzeliger's machine revolutionized the shoe-making industry by cutting the cost of producing shoes by 50 percent. This made it possible for the average person to afford a pair of shoes—maybe even two pairs. Yet, less than fifteen years after his death, most people didn't know Matzeliger was a black man.

An article written about the shoe-lasting machine falsely identified the inventor as white. In 1912, a researcher traced Matzeliger back to Lynn, where a certified copy of his death certificate was found. It stated Matzeliger was a mulatto—a term used to describe a person who had at least one black parent.

Matzeliger finally received the honor that was his due in 1991, when the United States Postal Service issued a commemorative stamp honoring him as an African American whose invention helped make life better for people all over the world.

*In the 1800s, railroads changed the face of America.
This 1870 poster advertises cross-country service in
just under seven days—amazing speed in those days.*

A BETTER LIFE, A BETTER WAY
Railroad Inventions

James Watt (1736–1819), the well-known Scottish inventor, patented an improvement of a steam-powered engine in 1769, thereby ushering in a new era of industrial development. In turn, inventors throughout the nineteenth century built on or improved upon his steam-powered engine. These improvements were never more evident than in the railroad industry.

On the Right Track

Between 1865 and 1900, the railroads employed more African Americans than any other industry. Blacks helped lay the tracks, and build and service the cars. They also took care of the passengers on board. The work was steady, but the salaries were poor, and the working conditions were often demeaning and dangerous. Railroad injuries were frequent and often fatal. One of the most dangerous places to work was in the train yards, where the cars were connected, until Andrew Jackson Beard (1859–1921) developed the "Jenny Coupler."

After the Civil War, Beard worked in an Alabama train yard, where men were often seriously injured and killed trying to attach train cars. A trainman had to be ready to drop a coupling pin in place as two cars rolled together. But sometimes a worker was crushed to death or lost a limb trying to do this. Beard studied the problems and developed a solution: an automatic device that allowed train cars to be put together quickly and safely. He patented it in 1897, but 6,500 other people who had designed coupling devices also obtained patents.

How could so many inventors receive patents on the same idea? More than one person can share the same idea, but the unique way an inventor *develops* that idea is what gets patented. Even though Beard had lots of competition, his design was so good, he was paid $50,000 by a company that began manufacturing his coupler. The "Jenny Coupler" helped save the lives of countless railroad workers.

The Real McCoy

Another inventor who started his career working for the railroads was Elijah McCoy (1843–1929). Have you ever heard the expression "the real McCoy?" This phrase originated with this inventor and his inventions.

Elijah McCoy patented dozens of inventions.

His automatic lubricators helped increase the safety and efficiency of engines. When cheap and inferior imitations of his designs flooded the market, customers, before making a purchase, began asking "Is this the real McCoy?" Today the question is synonymous with "Is this the best?"

McCoy was born in Colchester, Ontario, Canada, on May 2, 1843, the son of two runaway slaves. After the Civil War, Elijah's family moved to Ypsilanti, Michigan, where he attended school and worked in a machine shop. He was an alert, inquisitive child who liked to tinker with things. He wanted to attend engineering school, but there weren't too many educational opportunities open to him, so, at great sacrifice, his parents sent him to Edinburgh, Scotland, to study.

After finishing his apprenticeship in mechanical engineering, McCoy returned to the United States. Unfortunately, attitudes about African-American ability had not changed much. The only place that would hire McCoy was the Michigan Central Railroad. As a train fireman, McCoy was responsible for keeping the engine fueled and well-oiled. It was a hot, backbreaking job requiring more brawn than brains.

With lots of time to think on his job, McCoy was always looking for ways to improve his knowledge of machines. He noticed that engines of all types had to be stopped periodically and oiled or they would break down or catch fire. Often very young children were hired to work in factories for pennies a day as "oilers." Some were orphans who slept in the factories on the floor beneath the machinery. It was dirty, dangerous work, and the children were often maimed or killed. Seen climbing around on machines, these children were called "grease monkeys," a term still used today for mechanics.

McCoy knew that lubricating the engine was important, but stopping the train or the machine every time the engine needed to be oiled was costly and inefficient. There had to be a way for machines to be oiled while in operation. McCoy worked on the problem for two years, designing an automatic lubricating device. Finally, in July 1872, McCoy patented a "drip cup," the first of his automatic lubricating devices (patent #129,843). In his patent application, McCoy called

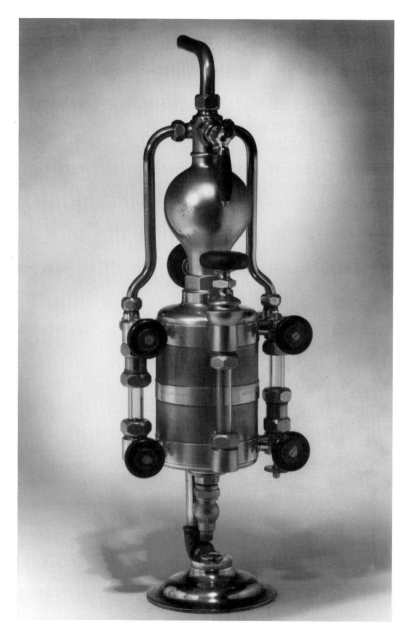

*This McCoy lubricator, patented in 1882,
was designed for locomotives.*

his invention an "Improvement in Lubricators for Steam-Engines." It worked in the following way: A cup filled with oil was attached to the machine, and a stop-cock regulated the flow of oil—while the engine was still running.

An Ypsilanti company was assigned the rights to manufacture the device, which was used on large, stationary factory equipment.

McCoy moved to Detroit, Michigan, where he worked as a consultant for a railroad conglomerate. During his career, he patented fifty-seven other designs, twenty-three of which were lubricating devices for various kinds of machines, including train engines. Although he worked for the Elijah McCoy Manufacturing Company in Detroit, McCoy didn't own any shares in the company. He died in 1929, but his name is remembered whenever consumers ask for the best—the real McCoy.

While Elijah McCoy was inventing the self-lubrication device, other people were at work in the new field of electricity.

LIGHTING THE WAY

Lewis Latimer

Like Elijah McCoy, Lewis Latimer (1848–1928) was the son of fugitive slaves, George and Rebecca Latimer. On October 4, 1842, the Latimers began a daring escape from Norfolk, Virginia, that ended in Boston, Massachusetts. Even in Boston, George Latimer was not safe because of the Fugitive Slave Law. He was arrested there, but antislavery leaders protested, and Latimer's freedom was purchased for $300.

Latimer's Early Life

The Latimers moved to Chelsea, Massachusetts, right outside Boston, where Lewis was born on September 4, 1848. He was the youngest of four children—he had two brothers and a sister. When Lewis was about ten years old, his father deserted the family. His mother found work as a stewardess on a ship, so she arranged for Lewis and his brother William to be sent to a farm school outside Boston. It was a harsh place where children were held until they could be hired out to employers. Lewis and William ran away from the school and made their way back to the city. There they found their oldest brother, who was taking care of himself. The two younger boys supported themselves, too, by doing odd jobs.

During the Civil War, both of Lewis's brothers joined the Union army, but Lewis was too young. Later, he lied about his age and enlisted in the navy on September 13, 1864. He served as a cabin boy on the USS *Massasoit*, a side-wheel gunboat, and saw action in several battles.

When the war ended, Latimer returned to Boston. He had no education, so finding a job was difficult. But since he had always been a good employee wherever he worked, he had good character references. Latimer was hired as an office boy with the firm of Crosby and Gould, patent lawyers.

Watching draftsmen making sketches of inventors' ideas, Latimer became interested in mechanical drawing. At night, he taught himself to do the detailed mechanical drawings required by the U.S. Patent Office. His employers gave him a job as a draftsman, and within a few years he was the chief draftsman there. By that time, the company was called Crosby and Gregory.

By working so closely with inventors and patent lawyers, Latimer learned how to apply for a patent. In 1874, he and W. C. Brown applied for and received a patent on an improved version of a "water closet" (bathroom) suitable for use on trains. That same year, Latimer met Alexander Graham Bell, who was then a teacher at a school for the deaf. Bell was working on an instrument through which sound could be carried by means of wires.

Latimer was the draftsman who did the detailed drawings for Bell's invention, and on March 7, 1876, Bell was granted a patent on the telephone.

Three years later, the firm Latimer worked for closed, and he was out of a job. He decided to look for work in Bridgeport, Connecticut, a booming industrial town. At this same time, Thomas Edison (1847–1931) had patented the electric light bulb, but the bulbs lasted only a few days before they burned out. There was a need to improve the efficiency of the light bulb so it would be more practical to manufacture and sell to the general public. Electric companies sprang up all over the world as the race was on to patent the "improvement" on Edison's light bulb. The person who could improve upon Edison's invention could make a fortune.

One of the competitors was Hiram S. Maxim, founder and chief electrician for the U.S. Electric Lighting Company. Maxim had worked for Crosby and Gould, and he gladly hired Latimer to be his assistant manager and draftsman. Latimer's new job placed him at the cutting edge of nineteenth-century electrical technology. Not since Watt's steam engine would an invention have such an impact on daily life.

Latimer's interest in electricity was not inspired by prospects of wealth or fame. He was motivated by the idea of harnessing electricity for practical use. In 1881,

Lewis Latimer was a pioneer in the field of electricity.

Fig. 1

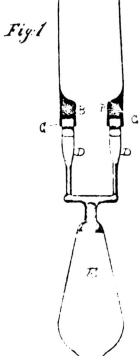

The electric lamp he designed with Joseph V. Nichols improved on earlier models.

Latimer and a co-worker, Joseph V. Nichols, improved the incandescent light bulb, which "transformed electric current into light through the invention of a durable, carbon filament." In 1882, Latimer received a patent on the process of manufacturing carbon filament, which causes a bulb to glow longer. This allowed Maxim to produce lamps less expensively and pass the savings on to consumers who could now afford to light their homes and businesses.

Maxim and his partner Charles Westin placed Latimer in charge of the installation of electric street lights in New York, Philadelphia, and other cities. Latimer also helped set up the production department of the Maxim-Westin Electric Light Company in London, England. (The company would later become known as Westinghouse.)

In 1883, Thomas Edison invited Latimer to join his company, which became General Electric. Edison was brilliant, some say even a genius, but Edison didn't think so. "There is no such thing as a genius," Edison quipped. "What people choose to call genius is simply hard work." Edison surrounded himself with people he respected for their skills and intellect regardless of race, sex, or creed. He worked hard and expected those he hired to work equally hard.

Latimer accepted Edison's offer. The following year, he began working in the engineering/product development department located in New Jersey. Several years later, Latimer was transferred to the legal department, where he worked on patents that were under dispute. He stayed in that department until 1896.

When Latimer wasn't testifying in court, he helped prepare cases and did patent searches in English,

French, and German, languages he had taught himself to read and write fluently.

Lewis Latimer had other interests besides electricity. He was a devoted husband and father who often stated he was happiest when sharing his leisure time with his wife Mary and their two daughters, Louise Rebecca and Emma Jeanette. He made time in his demanding schedule to teach English and mechanical drawing to immigrants, and he enjoyed writing poetry. No matter how busy he was, he found time to help others less fortunate. He said it was through the kindness of others that he had been helped.

A Social Conscience

Latimer counted among his friends Frederick Douglass, with whom he had corresponded for years. Douglass had been instrumental in helping raise the funds that were used to purchase George Latimer's freedom. In 1889, President Benjamin Harrison had appointed Douglass the minister to Haiti.

The Douglass-Latimer letters show that both men were concerned that the masses of blacks were still poor and uneducated, and therefore unable to fully enjoy their freedom. When Douglass died in February 1895, a strong and uncompromising voice for justice and equality for all was silenced. Latimer was saddened by his friend's death.

The inventor also knew Booker T. Washington, who by the 1890s had become a well-known educator. A few months after Douglass's death, Washington made his controversial "Atlanta Compromise" speech, in which he used the finger-fist analogy. Holding up his hand with fingers spread, he said that blacks and whites could be as separate as the fingers on the hand in all things social. Next, Washington made a fist and said that in matters of national interest, the races could be as united as the fist.

To blame Washington for the events that resulted in the segregation of the country is ludicrous, but there is no question that whites exploited the content of his speech for that purpose. While some blacks agreed with Washington, others felt he had excused segregationists and supplied them with the language to disenfranchise black people who were already losing the right to vote in many states. Conditions worsened, and within two years, on May 18, 1896, the United States Supreme Court ruled in the infamous *Plessy v. Ferguson* case that the races could be "separate but equal."

Not since the Dred Scott decision had a case been more devastating to African Americans. Although there were loud protests from blacks such as Ida B. Wells-Barnett, W. E. B. DuBois, T. Thomas Fortune, and Monroe Trotter, none of them was able to stop the attack on their civil rights.

Lewis Latimer did not join the outspoken critics of Booker T. Washington, but he did express deep concern about the issues of the day. In 1895 he wrote that there should be no separation of the races, and that "it is our duty to show our country, and the world, that we are looking to the interests of the country at large, when we protest against the crime and injustice meted out to any class or condition of our citizens."

Latimer also admired Washington, who had built

Tuskegee Institute from the ground up. The school was a tribute to black ingenuity, creativity, and perseverance. Washington's educational philosophy was similar to that of Latimer, who believed in the principles of hard work, thrift, honesty, discipline, and self-pride. Students who graduated from Tuskegee were trained to be skilled craftsmen such as bricklayers, carpenters, and stonemasons. By the 1890s, the students there were learning about electricity.

In 1890, Lewis Latimer had written *Incandescent Electric Lighting: A Practical Description of the Edison System.* Latimer's book was a balance between scholarly theories and hands-on practical application, which made it popular with manual-school educators like Charles Pierce at Tuskegee. His engineering classes used their skills to wire the campus for electricity, which was completed in 1898, the same year the Spanish-American War began and black and white men united to fight and die.

John Henrik Clarke, a well-known African-American historian, described Latimer's important role in the rapidly growing and highly competitive electrical industry at the turn of the century:

The two giant electrical companies at the time were General Electric and Westinghouse. They organized a Board of Patent Control and appointed Latimer Chief Draftsman and expert legal witness for this board. During this time he traveled widely gathering evidence against companies who ill-used the patents of Westinghouse and General Electric.

Latimer stayed with the Board of Patent Control from 1896 until 1911 when he moved to Flushing, New York, where he worked in semi-retirement as a patent consultant.

Although Lewis Latimer won many honors, he was proudest of being a charter member of the Edison Pioneers. This organization was founded in 1918 to acknowledge the men who were creators of the electric industry and who had worked with Edison. Latimer's certificate read:

LEWIS LATIMER
IS A MEMBER OF THE
EDISON PIONEERS
AN ASSOCIATION FORMED TO BRING TOGETHER IN
FRIENDLY INTERCOURSE THE MEN WHO HAVE BEEN
ASSOCIATED WITH MR. THOMAS ALVA EDISON AND
HIS INTERESTS IN THE UNITED STATES OF AMERICA
OR ABROAD, WHO DESIRE TO PAY TRIBUTE TO HIS
TRANSCENDENT GENIUS, TO BEAR TESTIMONY
TO HIS ACHIEVEMENTS, TO ACKNOWLEDGE THE
AFFECTION AND ESTEEM IN WHICH THEY HOLD HIM,
AND AS FAR AS LIES WITHIN THEIR POWER TO
DO GOOD DEEDS IN HIS NAME.

Lewis Latimer died in Flushing, New York, on December 11, 1928, after having lived a life that one historian said was "worthy of emulation." Truly this man born of slave parents was one of the most outstanding of American inventors.

Several of the patent cases in which Lewis Latimer testified involved an inventor named Granville T. Woods. Woods sued the Edison and Phelps Company twice for patent infringement and won both cases. Following the second suit, Thomas Edison offered Woods a job. Unlike Latimer, Woods decided to remain on his own.

Granville T. Woods became one of the most famous African-American inventors.

THE HUMAN DYNAMO
Granville T. Woods

In 1900 and again in 1913, the U.S. Patent Office did surveys to find out how many patents had been issued to African Americans. The report stated that there were "more than a thousand colored patents [issued], many of which appear to be of considerable importance." Among those listed as very important were the fifty or more patents issued to Granville T. Woods (1856–1910). Because of Woods's electrical and telegraphic inventions, some historians compare him to Edison. Almost all of them agree that Woods was perhaps the most celebrated African-American inventor of the nineteenth century.

Granville Woods was born free in Columbus, Ohio, on April 23, 1856, a few weeks after Booker T. Washington was born a slave in Virginia. The Woods family was poor, and young Granville had little opportunity to attend school. He apprenticed as a machinist and blacksmith, beginning at age ten as a bellows blower.

While still a teenager, he earned extra money to pay for his education in mechanics. When his family moved to Missouri in 1872, Woods was hired by the Iron Mountain Railroad as a fireman. Beginning in 1878, Woods worked as an engineer on the British steamer *Ironsides*. He returned to the United States and worked for two years on the Danville and Southern railroads. During this time, he learned firsthand how machines operated and how to repair or improve them.

On His Own

Woods applied for jobs as a mechanic, but no company would hire him for anything but lowly positions. Although he had more training and experience than most people, he was passed over for promotions.

For a while, Woods made the most out of these dead-end jobs, but he soon realized that if he was ever going to fulfill his dreams, he needed to take a bold step. He moved to Cincinnati, Ohio, and started his own business.

Woods joined the early pioneers who were fascinated by electricity and all its potential. Opportunities were wide open in this area of science and invention. However, after reading everything he could about the subject, Woods knew he needed to be better prepared to be able to compete in this field. He took night classes in mechanical engineering, with an emphasis on electricity.

In 1884, Woods patented his first two inventions: an improved steam boiler furnace and an improved telephone transmitter. The following year, he developed an "electrical apparatus for transmitting messages." Bell Telephone bought the rights to use it. Woods sold the rights to these early inventions and used the money to finance Woods Electric Company, located in Cincinnati. There, he researched, manufactured, and sold his own products.

One of Woods's telegraph inventions, patented as an "Induction Telegraph," made it possible for telegraphs to be sent between two moving trains. Another one of his inventions significantly improved the safety and efficiency of railroad transmissions. On the patent application, he described the invention as a "synchronous multiplex railway telegraph." It allowed a dispatcher to know where trains were located at all times. Woods stated that the purpose of his invention was to avert accidents "by keeping each train informed of the whereabouts of the one immediately ahead and following it. . . ."

Lucius Phelps and Thomas Edison had also developed a similar telegraph system, which resulted in a patent dispute that had to be settled in court. Twice the courts ruled in Woods's favor because he was able to prove that he held the rights to inventions claimed by Edison and Phelps. His victories earned him wide acclaim. After losing to Woods the second time, Edison offered him a job. Booker T. Washington invited Woods to teach at Tuskegee. Woods turned them both down, preferring to stay independent.

The *Catholic Tribune* of January 14, 1886, stated that Granville T. Woods was "the greatest colored inventor in the history of the race and equal, if not superior, to any inventor in the country." But Woods had only just begun his work.

In 1890, Woods closed down the manufacturing end of his business and moved to New York City. With the help of his brother, Lyates Woods, he became a full-time electrical inventor. Among his major successes were developing and improving devices and systems for the electric streetcar.

In the late 1800s, Woods designed several devices for electric streetcars such as this one, outside City Hall in Cincinnati.

His inventions and innovations helped improve the method of transferring electricity to streetcars more safely and efficiently, by means of a third rail. This allows the railroad car "to receive the electrical current while reducing friction." The method is still used in New York City's subway system. In 1901 Woods sold the invention to the Union Electric Company.

Between 1902 and 1905, Woods patented innovations on automatic air brakes, which he sold to the Westinghouse Air Brake Company of Pennsylvania. He also patented fifteen inventions for electric railways, and a still larger number for electrical control systems.

Woods died in 1910. Volume 1 of *The Journal of Negro History* summarized his contributions best:

There is no inventor of the colored race whose creative genius has covered quite so wide a field as that of Granville T. Woods, nor one whose achievements have attracted more universal attention and favorable comments from technical and scientific journals both in this country and abroad.

The breakthroughs in electrical engineering during the latter decades of the nineteenth century paved the way for twentieth-century inventions that built on the work of electrical pioneers. Just as the light bulb changed the country, so did the automobile. Three men who left their mark in this field are Garrett Morgan, Frederick McKinley Jones, and Richard B. Spikes.

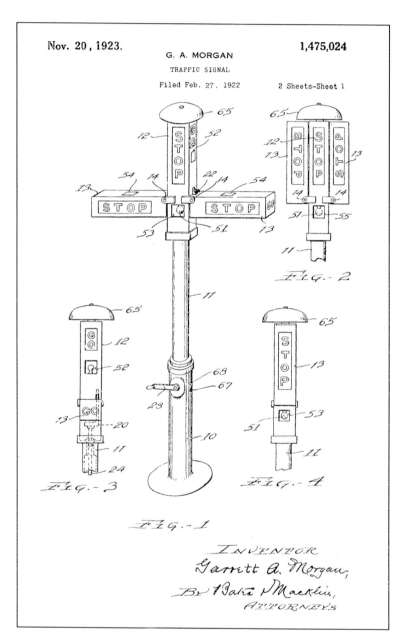

G. A. MORGAN

TRAFFIC SIGNAL

Filed Feb. 27. 1922

2 Sheets-Sheet 1

FIG. - 2

FIG. - 3

FIG. - 4

FIG. - 1

INVENTOR

Garrett A. Morgan,

By Baker Macklin,

ATTORNEYS

Garrett Morgan's traffic signal was the forerunner of today's traffic lights.

A STOP-AND-GO
PROPOSITION
Automotive Inventions

A basic scientific definition of an automobile is "a self-propelled land vehicle that can carry passengers." No one person "invented" the automobile. Scientists and inventors all over the world had been working on the concept since 1801, when Richard Trevithick constructed a mechanically powered vehicle in England. Even he was building on the work of others.

In the United States, automobile production increased after Henry Ford introduced vehicles that the average person could afford to own. By 1914, Ford motorcars were rolling off the first assembly lines.

Soon hundreds of thousands of people were working in the automotive industry, but the motorcar also created problems. Although there were stop signs at some corners, and police officers controlled the flow of traffic at major intersections, most motorists and pedestrians were confused about when they should stop, go, or move with caution. A whole new set of legal problems developed as well. Who had the right of way at an intersection? When and where was it safe for pedestrians to cross the street? In case of an accident, how was it determined who was at fault?

Gradually, local governments enacted traffic codes and ordinances to regulate city transportation. But it wasn't until Garrett Morgan developed the automatic street signal (patent #1,475,024) that driving became more manageable. He manufactured and distributed the signal for a while, but later sold it to the General Electric Company for $40,000, a considerable sum in the 1920s. It was from Morgan's design that today's familiar red, green, and yellow lights evolved. Morgan used the money to fund other worthwhile projects.

A Practical Dreamer

Garrett Morgan (1875–1963) began life as so many of his contemporaries did—in poverty. When he was fourteen years old, he dropped out of school and moved from Paris, Kentucky, to Cleveland, Ohio.

While working at a sewing-machine shop, Morgan became interested in machines. He was always looking for new and better answers to old problems. After a while, his family and friends began calling him a "practical dreamer." One of his earliest inventions was an improved sewing-machine part—a belt fastener. He sold the design for $150.

By 1909, Morgan had opened a small clothing manufacturing company (which employed over thirty people), had married, and had bought a house. Although he was a successful businessman, he still enjoyed inventing things.

For the most part, Morgan's inventions and innovations went unnoticed, until July 25, 1916. On that day, explosions ripped through a tunnel being built in Cleveland. Dozens of men were trapped under Lake Erie. Rescue efforts were set back by smoke, dust, and pockets of natural gas. The men were going to die if they didn't get help soon.

Someone remembered seeing Morgan demonstrate his new invention, a device called an "inhalator." He had designed and patented a gas mask in 1912 (patent #1,113,675). In 1914 he had won the grand prize at the 2nd International Exposition of Safety and Sanitation for his gas mask.

Morgan was contacted immediately after the explosion. He and his brother Frank soon arrived at the scene. The rescue workers watched in amazement as the Morgan brothers put on their inhalators— hoodlike devices that filtered the air—and descended into the tunnel 5 miles out and 282 feet under Lake Erie. Much to everyone's surprise and joy, the Morgans returned with an unconscious man. He was bruised and hurt, but alive! They returned to the tunnel and brought out another man. Volunteers joined the Morgans and, working all night, they brought other trapped men to safety. The Morgans were awarded a gold medal by the city of Cleveland for their heroism.

News of the success of Morgan's inhalator spread quickly. Orders poured in from fire departments, chemists, engineers, miners, and others who needed a

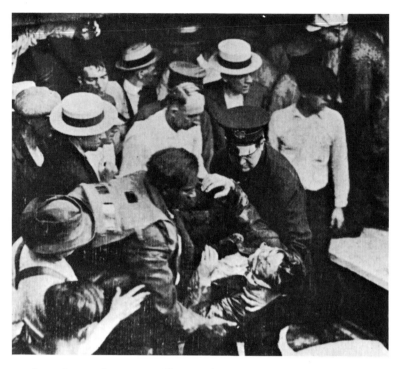

In a dramatic rescue, Garrett Morgan used his inhalator to save tunnel workers trapped beneath Lake Erie.

respiratory device. The National Safety Device Company, which Morgan had formed, had a reputation for being dependable. However, racism and discrimination were so prevalent at the time that the orders dropped off when it was discovered that Morgan was an African American.

When poison gas was used as a weapon during World War I, the federal government expressed an interest in Morgan's inhalator. He lost out to competitors because his device was considered too bulky. But he continued to produce his inhalator, which saved the lives of millions.

Morgan also patented a hair straightener called G.A. Morgan Hair Refining Cream. Some years earlier, two women inventors, Madam C. J. Walker and Annie Malone, had developed hair products for the African-American woman. In fact, Madam Walker had become the first American woman—black or white—to become a self-made millionaire.

For several years, Garrett Morgan published a newspaper, *The Cleveland Call*. He remained an active member of his community until he died in 1963 after a long and productive life. The world was a better place for the contributions he had made.

Throughout the early decades of the twentieth century, new and exciting designs and uses were developed for the motor vehicle. Trucks were used to transport goods from coast to coast. Buses were designed to carry people, and more specifically, the school bus was designed to transport children. Therefore, safety was a primary concern.

By the late 1950s, the nation had changed with regard to segregation. In 1954, the Supreme Court had made a landmark decision in the *Brown v. Board of Education* case, striking down the "separate but equal" doctrine. The walls of segregation were crumbling. Schools were ordered to desegregate "with all deliberate speed." Some states, like Missouri, integrated their schools the following year. Other states, like Arkansas and Alabama, resisted integration and dragged out the process in long court battles. Schools were supposed to be integrated, but the neighborhoods weren't. Therefore, the courts ordered busing. This decision raised many issues that are still being debated, but on a day-to-day basis, one of the concerns was: How safe are the buses that transport schoolchildren? Once again, inventors went to work in an effort to make buses safer.

Self-Taught Inventors

In January 1962, Richard B. Spikes, a Texan, developed and patented automatic safety brakes that combined both hydraulic and electrical systems. This made the brakes safer and more efficient on buses. Spikes, who was then legally blind, died a few months later.

Born in the late 1800s, Spikes was a self-taught mechanical engineer. One of his first inventions was a beer keg tap, patented in 1910 and bought by the Milwaukee Brewing Company. He also developed automatic directional lights, which were first installed in the Pierce Arrow automobile in 1913. Today all motor vehicles are equipped with blinking lights that show the direction a driver is going to turn.

Spikes's improvements of automobile transmissions and automatic gear-shifting devices were sold for over $100,000, one of the highest figures paid to a black inventor prior to the 1930s.

By 1961, Spikes was losing his sight, but he was determined to continue his work. He invented a drafting machine for the blind, then went on to complete the work on his "fail-safe" braking system (patent #3,015,522).

Most of the fresh and frozen foods we eat are brought to the market in refrigerated trucks. Frederick

McKinley Jones (1893 or 1892–1961) invented the first practical truck refrigeration system in the world.

Jones, orphaned soon after his birth in Cincinnati, Ohio, dropped out of school at age ten. He moved to Covington, Kentucky, where he was raised by a priest until about the age of sixteen. During that time, he worked at a bowling alley and at a construction job. Then he began working at a garage. By age nineteen, he was the shop foreman and an excellent mechanic. In his spare time, Jones built and raced cars he constructed from spare parts.

Jones served in the army during World War I, where he also studied electricity. Once the war was over, he moved to Hallock, Minnesota, where he was hired by Joseph A. Numero, the owner of a company that manufactured motion picture sound equipment.

In 1939, Jones patented his first design: a ticket-dispensing machine for movie houses (patent #2,163,754).

One day Jones overheard his boss discussing a problem with a truck driver. A load of chickens had spoiled because the ice had melted before the driver had gotten to his destination. Jones became interested in solving that problem.

By the 1930s, the refrigeration process had already been patented, so the inventor studied everything that was available on the subject. Then, using salvage parts and adding his experiences as a race-car builder, he slowly began to construct an air-cooling system that could withstand the rigors of transportation. It took Jones many years, but he was finally successful in 1949. The U.S. Patent Office awarded him a patent for his invention (patent #2,475,841). He and Numero formed a partnership and began marketing the air-cooling units. Their company, the Thermo King Corporation, grossed over $3 million by 1950.

Because of Jones's inventions, food and other perishable items could be transported inexpensively and the savings passed on to consumers. Later, Jones's refrigeration systems were used by the United States military to set up field kitchens and to store blood plasma. Railroad boxcars and, later, airplanes were equipped with a modified version of his invention.

Jones was accepted as a member of the American Society of Refrigeration Engineers. During the 1950s, he was used as a consultant on projects that required his expertise. When he died in 1961, Jones had been awarded over forty refrigeration patents, all of which helped to better the quality of American life.

———

Garrett Morgan, Richard Spikes, and Frederick Jones were all self-taught men who nevertheless set the standard by which inventors of their generation were measured. As educational and employment opportunities opened up for blacks, a new group of highly trained engineers emerged. Among them were men like Walter Daniel, the first black to earn a Ph.D. in engineering from the University of Iowa in 1932, and Elbert Cox, the first African American to earn a Ph.D. in pure mathematics from Cornell University in 1925. They both became teachers who, in turn, inspired men like Meredith Gourdine.

THE SKY IS
THE LIMIT

Contemporary Inventors and Their Inventions

Meredith Gourdine was born in Livingston, New Jersey, on the eve of the Great Depression in 1929—the same year Martin Luther King, Jr., was born. Economic times were hard during the 1930s, but Gourdine was encouraged to set goals and to work toward them. He attended a Catholic elementary school in Harlem in New York City, and graduated from Brooklyn Tech High School. Gourdine was also an excellent athlete.

While a student at Cornell University, Gourdine, nicknamed "Flash," earned a spot on the U.S. Olympic track team, and won a silver medal in the broad jump at the 1952 Olympic Games held in Helsinki, Finland.

While studying for his advanced degree in engineering physics at California Institute of Technology, Gourdine worked as a research scientist for several major corporations, including Caltech Jet Propulsion Lab, Plasmodyne Corporation, and the aeronautical division of Curtiss-Wright Corporation. After receiving his Ph.D. in 1960, Gourdine decided to form his own company, Gourdine Laboratories, in Livingston, New Jersey. His major interest was electrogas dynamics, which is the study of forces produced by charged particles (called ions) transmitted by gas flowing through an electric field. Fluorescent light bulbs, for example, use the process of electrogas dynamics (EGD).

In 1966, Gourdine was awarded a $600,000 government contract to complete work on an EGD generator that could produce energy less expensively and with far less pollution. His generator had no moving parts and didn't require steam. Gourdine Labs developed and patented many different products for many different purposes, including sea-water purification, refrigeration, heating and lighting homes, and automobile exhaust systems. Gourdine Labs developed and manufactured an "incineraid," a device that reduces the pollution caused by smoke from incinerators.

Though blind in his later years, Dr. Gourdine remained very interested in electrogas dynamics as a source of low-cost, efficient, and environmentally safe energy production.

More African-American Inventors

Other contemporary inventors include Otis Boykin (1920–1982) and Lloyd A. Hall (1894–1971). Boykin,

*As a graduate student in 1958, Meredith Gourdine
works on an experiment for his doctoral thesis.*

born in Dallas, Texas, was educated at Fisk University in Nashville, Tennessee, and Illinois Institute of Technology. He invented an electrical device used in all guided missiles and in the I.B.M. computer. He also developed an air filter and twenty-six other electronic devices, including a control unit used in heart stimulators or pacemakers. His invention has saved the lives of many people, but not his own. Dr. Boykin died in Chicago of heart failure at the age of sixty-two.

Lloyd Hall was born in Elgin, Illinois, in June 1894. He earned his undergraduate degree in pharmaceutical chemistry at Northwestern University and began working for the Chicago Health Department in 1916. He became interested in food chemistry, and in 1922 joined the staff of chemists at Boyer Griffith Laboratories. He remained at Griffith until he retired in 1959. During that time, Hall developed an improved method of preserving meats and other food products.

One of the most scholarly scientist-inventors of the twentieth century was J. Ernest Wilkins, Jr. He was born in Chicago in 1923 and graduated from the University of Chicago with Phi Beta Kappa honors just short of his seventeenth birthday. By age nineteen, he had earned his Ph.D. in mathematics. After teaching at Tuskegee Institute for a year, he joined the Manhattan Project during the early development of the atomic bomb. Later, while working for various major corporations, he invented a shield against gamma rays, and he later became a professor of mathematical physics at Howard University in Washington, D.C.

James C. Evans (1900–1992) was a graduate engineer and lawyer. During World War II, he served as an assistant civilian aide to the secretary of war. He later

*Physicist J. Ernest Wilkins, Jr., was
involved in the early development
of the atomic bomb.*

invented and patented a device that utilizes exhaust gases to prevent icing on aircraft.

Dr. Robert Bayless became a pioneer in the new field of microencapsulation. Bayless used the process to develop a carbonless paper, but applications of the process are infinite.

James Parsons, Jr., a graduate of Rensselaer Polytechnic Institute, became one of the most renowned metallurgists in the country. When Dr. Parsons was about twenty-seven, he became the chief chemist and metallurgist of the Duriron Company in Dayton, Ohio. He patented various corrosion-resistant alloy steels. During the 1960s, Dr. Parsons taught at Tennessee State University and inspired a generation of engineers who are now meeting the challenges of an ever-changing world.

Just as African-American inventors made significant contributions in the past, there is no doubt they will continue to do so in the future. More than ever before, black scientists, engineers, and inventors are part of research teams within large corporations. But some individuals are independently developing and improving ideas in their own basements and garage workshops.

In the near future, professions like computer medicine, robotics, and space gardening will be commonplace. As we all explore the outer regions of space, the ocean depths, and our inner selves, black inventors will be present, standing on the shoulders of the giants who paved the way for them. It is exciting to imagine all the possible inventions and innovations they will create.

BIBLIOGRAPHY

BOOKS

Adams, Russell L. *Great Negroes Past and Present*. Chicago: Afro-Am Publishing Company, 1984.

Aptheker, Herbert. *A Documentary History of the Negro People in the United States.*, vols. 1, 2, 3, and 4. New York: Citadel Press, 1973, Carol Publishing Group, 1990.

Asimov, Isaac. *The Wall Chart of Science and Invention: The Growth of Human Knowledge from Pre-History to Space Travel*. New York: Macmillan, 1992.

Bennett, Lerone, Jr. *Before the Mayflower: A History of Black America*, 6th ed. Chicago: Johnson Publishing, 1988.

Burt, McKinley, Jr. *Black Inventors of America*. Portland, Oregon: National Book Company, 1989.

Carwell, Hattie. *Blacks in Science: Astrophysicist to Zoologist*. Smithtown, NY: Exposition Press, 1977.

DeForest, Thomas E. *Inventor's Guide to Successful Patent Applications*. Blue Ridge Summit, PA: Tab Books, Inc., 1988.

Haber, Louis. *Black Pioneers of Science and Invention*. New York: Harcourt Brace Jovanovich, 1970.

James, Portia P. *The Real McCoy: African-American Invention and Innovation, 1619–1930*. Washington, D.C.: Smithsonian Press, 1989.

Sammons, Vivian Ovelton. *Blacks in Science and Medicine*. New York: Hemisphere Publishing, 1990.

Van Sertima, Ivan, ed. *Blacks in Science Ancient and Modern*. New Brunswick, NJ: Journal of African Civilizations Ltd., 1983.

Williams, James C. *At Last Recognition in America*, vol. 1, *A Reference Handbook of Unknown Black Inventors and Their Contributions to America*. Chicago: B.C.C. Publishing, 1978.

ARTICLES

"Sketches of a Few Greats and Near Greats." *The Afro-American History Kit*. Washington, D.C.: Associated Publishers, 1992.

INDEX

ABOUT THE
AUTHORS

Patricia and Fredrick McKissack are well-known authors of children's books. Among their many acclaimed nonfiction works are numerous biographies, including *Sojourner Truth: Ain't I a Woman*, and *The Civil Rights Movement in America from 1865 to the Present*, a history that is used in junior high and middle schools all over the country. In 1990, the McKissacks combined their talents to write *A Long Hard Journey: The Story of the Pullman Porter*, which won both the Coretta Scott King Award and the Jane Addams Peace Award. They have also written beginning-reader and picture books, and have served as editors for several series. Among Patricia's well-received books are *Jesse Jackson: A Biography* and *The Dark-Thirty: Southern Tales of the Supernatural*. Both McKissacks are 1964 Tennessee State graduates, and Pat earned a master's degree in early childhood education at Webster University in St. Louis, Missouri. The McKissacks live in St. Louis.